Early Childhood Education: What Research Tells Us

Lilian G. Katz

**PHI DELTA KAPPA
EDUCATIONAL FOUNDATION**

LILIAN G. KATZ

Lilian G. Katz is professor of Early Childhood Education at the University of Illinois, where she also serves as director of the ERIC Clearinghouse on Elementary and Early Childhood Education. A native of Great Britain, she immigrated to the United States in 1947 and graduated from Woodrow Wilson High School in Los Angeles. She earned her B.A. from San Francisco State University and her Ph.D. from Stanford University in 1968.

Katz began her professional career as a nursery school teacher. She currently teaches graduate courses in early childhood education and an advanced course on research in teacher educaton. She has been a visiting professor in Canada, England, Australia, West Germany, India, Barbados, and the People's Republic of China. In 1988 she was a Visiting Fellow at the Froebel Institute in London.

In addition to extensive publications in journals and books, Katz serves as editor-in-chief of the *Early Childhood and Research Quarterly* and writes a monthly column on early childhood education in *Parents Magazine*.

Series Editor, Derek L. Burleson

Early Childhood Education: What Research Tells Us

by
Lilian G. Katz

Library of Congress Catalog Card Number 88-61705
ISBN 0-87367-280-1
Copyright © 1988 by the Phi Delta Kappa Educational Foundation
Bloomington, Indiana

This fastback is sponsored by the University of Illinois Chapter of Phi Delta Kappa, which made a generous contribution toward publication costs.

In celebration of its 75th Anniversary in 1989, the University of Illinois Chapter sponsors this fastback in honor of all members past and present for their 75 years of continuous service to the profession.

LB
1140.2
.K368
1988

Table of Contents

Trends in Early Childhood Education 7
   Curriculum Trends 8

**Implications of Recent Research for the Early
Childhood Curriculum** 9
   The Concept of Development 10
   The Role of Interactive Learning 12

Four Categories of Learning 14
   Fostering the Four Categories of Learning 15

Risks of Academic Pressures on Young Children 18
   Variety of Teaching Methods 19
   Learned Stupidity 20
   Informal Learning Environment 20

The Development of Interest 21
   Effects of Rewards and Feedback on Interest 21
   Confusing Self-Esteem with Narcissism 23
   Time for Learning 24

Developing Communicative Competence 25

Developing Social Competence 27
   The Recursive Cycle 28

Curriculum Options 30
   Characteristics of Projects 30
   The School Bus Project 31

References 34

MAY 1 2 1992

Gottman, J.M. "How Children Become Friends." *Monographs of the Society for Research in Child Development* 48, no. 3 (1983). Serial No. 201.

Hitz, R., and Wright, D. "Kindergarten Issues: A Practitioner's Survey." *Principal* 67, no. 5 (1988): 28-31.

Kagan, S.L. "Early Schooling: On What Grounds?" In *Early Schooling: The National Debate*, edited by S.L. Kagan and E.F. Zigler. New Haven, Conn.: Yale University Press, 1987.

Katz, L.G., and Chard, S.C. *Engaging Children's Minds: The Project Approach*. Norwood, N.J.: Ablex, forthcoming.

Katz, L.G.; Raths, J.D.; and Torres, R. *A Place Called Kindergarten*. Urbana, Ill.: ERIC Clearinghouse on Elementary and Early Childhood Education, 1986.

National Association for the Education of Young Children. "NAEYC Position Statement on Standardized Testing of Young Children 3 Through 8 Years of Age." *Young Children* (March 1988): 42-47.

Parker, J., and Asher, S. "Peer Relations and Later Personal Adjustment: Are Low-Accepted Children at Risk?" *Psychological Bulletin* 102, no. 3 (1987): 357-89.

Rosenfield, E.; Folger, R.; and Adelman, H.F. "When Rewards Reflect Competence: A Qualification of the Overjustification Effect." *Journal of Personality and Social Psychology* 39, no. 3 (1980): 368-76.

Schweinhart, L. "How Important Is Child-Initiated Activity?" *Principal* 67, no. 5 (1988): 6-10.

Tuchscherer, P. *TV Interactive Toys: The New High Tech Threat to Children*. Bend, Ore.: Pinnaroo, 1988.

Wells, M. "The Roots of Literacy." *Psychology Today* (June 1988): 20-22.

Wertsch. J.V., ed. *Culture, Communication, and Cognition: A Vygotskian Perspective*. New York: Cambridge University Press, 1985.

References

Bredekamp, S., ed. *Developmentally Appropriate Practice in Early Childhood Programs Serving Children from Birth Through Age 8.* Washington, D.C.: NAEYC, 1987.

Bruner, J.S., and and Haste, H.W. "Introduction." In *Making Sense: The Construction of the Child's World*, edited by J.S. Bruner and H.W. Haste. New York: Methuen, 1987.

Burton, C. "Problems in Children's Peer Relations: A Broadening Perspective." In *Current Topics in Early Childhood Education*, edited by L.G. Katz. Vol. 7. Norwood, N.J.: Ablex, 1987.

Center for Education Statistics. *Condition of Education*. Washington, D.C.: U.S. Government Printing Office, 1985.

Day, B.D. "What's Happening in Early Childhood Programs Across the United States." In *A Resource Guide to Public School Early Childhood Programs*, edited by C. Warger. Alexandria, Va.: Association for Supervision and Curriculum Development, 1988.

Deci, E.L., and Ryan, R.M. *Intrinsic Motivation and Self-Determination in Human Behavior*. New York: Plenum, 1985.

Dweck, C.S. "Motivational Processes Affecting Learning." *American Psychologist* 41, no. 10 (1986): 1040-48.

Dweck, C.S., and Leggett, E.L. "A Social-Cognitive Approach to Motivation And Personality." *Psychological Review* 95, no. 2 (1988): 256-73.

Gallagher, J.M., and Coche, J. "Hothousing: The Clinical and Educational Concerns over Pressuring Young Children." *Early Childhood Research Quarterly* 2, no. 3 (1987): 203-11.

of how it works, and what features of it contribute to their safety. And what is especially important is that the project provided a context in which children's dispositions to observe, inquire, and become interested and involved in a sustained group effort were strengthened.

In a project of this type the teacher can engage children in a wide range of interesting activities that will take several days or even weeks of continuous probing and exploring. They can ask questions of adults other than their teacher; for example, the bus driver and perhaps a mechanic. They can look up things in reference books of appropriate levels of difficulty. Because the children are expected to, and want to, explain what they have learned to their classmates, they are likely to persist in obtaining information and communicating it with understanding. Furthermore, for many of the children in the class, this project is likely to strengthen the disposition to observe all kinds of vehicles more closely than they had before, perhaps making useful comparisons and reporting them to their classmates from time to time.

In sum, the project approach can be valuable for young children because it addresses their intellects, strengthens a variety of important dispositions, provides opportunities to apply basic skills, offers rich content for conversation, and uses a meaningful context for peer interaction and cooperative effort. Projects are also culturally relevant in that they focus on the children's own interests and environments. Project work does not have to constitute the whole of the curriculum, but it should be one of the important informal aspects of the curriculum. Then, as children get older, more of their time can be allocated to formal instructional work (Katz and Chard, forthcoming).

Not to be overlooked in the project approach is that it can make teaching interesting — something unlikely to be true of more formal, academic approaches to early childhood education.

some lights flash, some are simply reflectors; some are white, some red, and some amber. Another group might study the gauges and dials on the dashboard and learn what kinds of information they yield. Another group might concentrate on math activities such as measuring the width of the bus, counting the number of seats and wheels, and learning something about air pressure in the tires. Two children might examine the inside and outside rear-view mirrors.

Imagine the rich vocabulary building that can come from this project, with such terms as ignition, emergency door, fuel, dial, gauge, air pressure, accelerator, rear-view mirror, gears, emergency exit, seating capacity, etc. Those children able to do so could copy down all the words they could find on the bus and use the vocabulary for "writing" and reading their own stories. The door of a school bus, usually opened and closed with a lever, is unlikely to resemble those at home or in school. Thus, varieties of doors in their immediate environment might become a topic for extended study. Or the project might extend to an investigation of the route taken by the bus, who and how many children board at each stop, what traffic signs and signals are passed en route, etc.

According to my source, after the children had carried out their detailed examination of the bus, they built a bus from scrap materials in their classroom and then acted out a variety of roles associated with transporting children from home to school and back, including managing traffic at intersections and handling rowdy passengers. Virtually all aspects of the work undertaken by the children in this project could lend themselves to artwork including drawing, painting, and making plasticene or wooden models.

The purpose of selecting the school bus as a project for these young children was not to achieve some grandiose cognitive goal. Heaven forbid that these children will ever have to take a standardized test on their knowledge of school buses! Rather, what is important is that the bus was part of their daily environment. They learned a lot about it: the correct names of various parts of it, a simple understanding

project. When children are encouraged to select the topic and initiate the activities to carry out the project, long-term benefits to their development follow (Schweinhart 1988). A project should also provide opportunities for children to apply the skills they already have or are just beginning to learn. In a sense, a project is an integrated curriculum allowing children to apply all the basic skills as they carry out the various activities.

The younger the children, the more important it is that the project has the potential for expressive activity and for interaction, such as role playing, block building, or other kinds of construction. An appropriate project for the early years is one that deepens children's understandings of events and objects around them and concerns matters with which they have direct and firsthand experience. Project topics also should have more *horizontal* relevance than *vertical* relevance. Horizontal relevance means that what the children are learning about and learning to do is relevant to their experiences outside of the school setting. Vertical relevance means that what the children are learning is preparing them for the next level of schooling. While both kinds of relevance are important, the younger the children, the more the emphasis should be on horizontal relevance in the selection of project topics and activities.

The School Bus Project

An example of a project that incorporates many of the good practices discussed above is one I recently heard about involving a class of kindergartners who undertook a detailed study of their own school bus. Although I did not observe the project in operation, it is easy to imagine the kinds of activities the children might have undertaken. One small group might study the driving mechanism including the motor, gear shift, brakes, accelerator, steering wheel, etc. Another group might study the variety of lights inside and outside the bus. The children would learn that some lights are for signals, others are to give warnings, and some, of course, are to light the way ahead;

Curriculum Options

Many people within and outside the early childhood field tend to view the curriculum in either/or terms. The choice should be either an academic focus or a free-play socialization focus. Some of the risks of prematurely introducing academic tasks to young children have already been discussed. But the alternative to an academic focus is not simply to provide spontaneous play and creative activities (although all children up to about age seven or eight can probably benefit from regular opportunities for spontaneous play). Rather, the data on children's learning seem to suggest that what is required is an *intellectual* focus, which engages children's minds as they interact in small groups while working together on a variety of projects. These projects should also strengthen their dispositions to observe, experiment, inquire, and reconstruct aspects of their environment (Katz and Chard, forthcoming).

Characteristics of Projects

A project is an in-depth study or investigation that a group of children undertake on a particular topic or theme. It might be a study of the local supermarket, a neaby fishing harbor, or an adjacent construction site. Unlike spontaneous play, projects involve children in planning and activities requiring sustained effort over a period of days or weeks, depending on the age of the children and the nature of the

to try out and by encouraging them to experiment with constructive approaches to their peers.

Recent research suggests that if teachers, parents, and other adults help children develop their social competence in the early years, they can do a great deal to establish positive recursive cycles in children and relieve much of the anguish that inevitably comes in later years from negative cycles. These recent insights from research on children's social competence suggest that preschool teachers' concern with social development is well placed and should be given as much weight in the curriculum as children's intellectual development. The research also implies that young children should be engaged in activities in which cooperation and group efforts are functional, not contrived.

instruction or even coaching. However, maladaptive patterns can be modified by a knowledgeable teacher, using a variety of intervention techniques that have been tested in experimental and clinical studies. These studies suggest a range of approaches that teachers can use to foster the development of social competence in the early years (Burton 1987).

The Recursive Cycle

It is useful to think of social competence as a recursive cycle, in which reactions to an individual's given behavior patterns tend to increase the chances that the same behavior patterns will be repeated or sustained. For example, children who are likable, attractive, and friendly tend to elicit positive responses from others. And because they receive such positive responses, they become more likeable, attractive, and friendly. Their appealing qualities also result in increased opportunities to polish the social skills they have and to acquire new ones. Similarly, children who are unattractive, unfriendly, and difficult to like tend to be avoided or rejected. In response to this avoidance and rejection, they tend to behave in ways that make them even more unattractive, often repeating the very behavior that causes even stronger rejection. Thus in cyclic fashion, the behavior tends to feed on itself. At the same time the opportunities for such children to strengthen whatever social skills they might have, and to learn new ones, are gradually diminished. As a result, the behavior patterns causing rejection become well established.

Young children cannot break a negative cycle by themselves. Even adults have difficulty breaking a dysfunctional cycle of social behavior. Because young children have little capacity for understanding the causes of their dysfunctional behaviors, they cannot infer what corrections and adjustments are necessary to overcome them. Adults must intervene to break the recursive cycle. Teachers can do this in the early childhood setting by suggesting specific strategies for children

Developing Social Competence

The evidence is now very compelling that young children who fail to achieve minimal social competence by the time they are about six, give or take a year, are at significant risk as adults. They are at risk in terms of their future mental health and, some say, even in terms of marital adjustment, parenting competence, and ultimate occupational adjustment (Gottman 1983). Research also shows that children who are not accepted or who are aggressive have a strong likelihood of being school dropouts and of becoming delinquents (Parker and Asher 1987).

Although definitions of social competence vary on some details, they generally include the capacity to initiate, develop, and maintain satisfying relationships with others, especially peers. This does not mean a child should be a social butterfly; there is no reason for concern if a child chooses to work or play alone, as long as he or she is capable of interacting successfully with others when it is desired and appropriate.

The acquisition of social competence involves many complex interactions beginning in early infancy. From these interactions children learn both appropriate and inappropriate social responses. Inappropriate responses may be intensified during such interactions unless adults help children to alter maladaptive behavior patterns. In the preschool period, children's social interaction skills are barely under conscious control and are unlikely to be improved through direct

children were learning to "listen," but many appeared to be learning to "tune out" their stammering classmates.

Conversations are more likely to be prolonged when adults make responses to children's expressions than when they ask them questions (Katz and Chard, forthcoming). Unfortunately, many adults use the kind of interrogation question with children for which the questioner already knows the answer. The child's task then becomes one of trying to figure out what answer is expected. A constant flow of interrogatory questions tends to be intimidating and even threatening at times.

Children's engagement in conversation is supported when teachers make benign but friendly comments like, "Yes, I see what you mean," or "I've been there (or felt that way, or noticed that), too," or "That's true," or something that is equally simple but, nevertheless, reflects genuine interest in what the child is saying. The relevant principle of practice for fostering communicative competence is that that the younger the child, the more the teacher uses small-group and one-to-one conversations and avoids too much one-way communication to the entire class.

Developing Communicative Competence

Early childhood is a critical period in the development of communicative competence, which includes self-expression, understanding and communicating with others, and verbal reasoning. Children today are exposed to language in many forms (some of which they could do without), but the development of communicative competence requires that children be engaged in *conversation*, not simply be exposed passively to language.

Conversations with adults and other children strengthen all the communicative competencies. Conversations are a sequential string of interactions in which the content of each participant's contribution is contingent on the content of the contributions of the other. But it takes about seven years for children to acquire basic conversational skills.

Conversations are more likely to occur when children are working or meeting in small groups — with or without an adult. Experienced teachers of young children recognize the futility of carrying on conversation with an entire class. Novice teachers expend much effort reminding their pupils that someone else is still speaking or that their turn has not yet come! Conversations are more likely to occur when there is something of genuine interest to the children to talk about. I watched a kindergarten teacher attempting to engage a class of five-year-olds in a discussion by asking each in turn, "What is your news today?" Each child struggled to find something headline-worthy to report to disinterested squirming classmates. Perhaps some of these

One of the major roles of teachers is to deepen children's interest in and understanding of things around them that are worth learning more about. Self-esteem develops in the course of interacting with significant others at home, in the community, in one's ethnic group, as well as in the classroom. It can be strengthened through undertaking challenging tasks, overcoming obstacles, and helping others. It is not strengthened through such gimmicks as buttons that say, "I'm Special." Such gimmicks, if they have any effect at all, tend to increase self-centeredness, rather than involvement in outside interests. The cumulative effects of frequent flattery and self-referencing borders on narcissism.

Time for Learning

One of the current problems in the early childhood curriculum is the fragmentation of children's time for work. Children seem to be constantly hurried to complete a task and move to the next activity. Teachers find themselves saying, "Finished or not, it's time to go on to gym (or music, or computer, or art, or whatever)." A daily schedule that allots a specified number of minutes for each activity is bound to result in fragmentation. The daily time allocation for various activities should allow for flexibility. The relevant principle of practice here for strengthening the interest disposition is that children need opportunities to engage in activities that call for sustained effort and extended work over time (days or weeks) on topics that interest them.

Attempts to provide children with constant amusement and excitement also risk undermining the development of interest dispositions. The choice facing teachers is not workbooks and worksheets versus macaroni collages and pasting pre-cut leaves on construction paper. None of these activities is sufficiently mind-engaging to develop children's interest dispositions. What is needed are opportunities for the children to engage in projects that call for extension, elaboration, and continuation of work and play over several days or weeks. Project work provides the kinds of experiences that cultivate and strengthen interest disposition.

Over the past 25 years or so, teachers have been inundated with professional literature telling them about the importance of positive reinforcement for fostering children's self-esteem. Teachers may now have reached the point of overdoing the amount of general positive feedback they give. However, if teachers are to make their feedback specific and informative, they cannot offer it every two minutes. It would be impossible to identify pertinent information and to comment on it at that pace. Thus the relevant principle of practice here is that teachers should reduce the frequency of general feedback; but when feedback is given, it should be informative. Maria Montessori understood this principle of teaching intuitively when she enjoined teachers not to be intrusive. Too many rewards and too frequent praise can be distracting to children and get in the way of their spontaneous interest and break their concentration and involvement. However, we must remember that concentration and involvement come only when children have mind-engaging activities available to them.

Confusing Self-Esteem with Narcissism

Teachers are told that they must enhance young children's self-esteem in every way possible. But observation and experience in many early childhood classrooms suggests widespread confusion between enhancing self-esteem and promoting narcissism. Some efforts to enhance children's self-esteem take the form of preoccupation with self and how one appears to others. This is a form of narcissism. For example, young children are often given buttons or pins to wear that say, "I'm Important" or "I'm Special." Another example is a first-grade class in which every child was expected to create a little book titled "All About Me." Each of the dittoed pages to be filled in by a child covered such topics as "What I like to eat," "What I like to watch on television," "What I want for a present," "Where I want to go on vacation." Every one of the pages was essentially a consumer activity dealing with the child's own acquisitiveness. There was no page that said, "What I am curious about," "What I want to learn more about."

wards for those activities young children seem to enjoy spontaneously. To the child, the reward signals that the task is over, and his disposition to continue to think about it and return to it voluntarily is weakened.

This does not mean rewards are never appropriate; it means that they must be used sparingly and in the appropriate context. Once children are exposed to a steady stream of extrinsic rewards for every task they undertake, they may become "hooked" on them. By the time they are adolescents, the cumulative effect of constant extrinsic rewards could be that with every task or assignment they will ask, "What's in it for me?" or "What do I get for doing it?" The disposition of intrinsic interest and motivation is lost.

A parallel line of research on the effects of positive feedback on children's interest suggests that different kinds of feedback affect interest and motivation in different ways. It appears that positive feedback of a *general* nature may serve to increase children's productivity but not their interest. In other words, children will continue to produce in order to get positive feedback but will abandon the task when the feedback is withdrawn. General positive feedback includes such vague comments from the teacher as "very good," "well done," or "smiley" faces and gold stars stuck on children's papers.

On the other hand, if the positive feedback is *specific*, particularly if it includes information about the competence of the work, it serves to strengthen interest (Rosenfield, Folger, and Adelman 1980). Academically oriented programs typically emphasize general positive feedback, ostensibly to give children feelings of success and to spur productivity. This strategy appears to work well for coercing young children to keep working at often trivial tasks. But when children receive positive feedback that is *informative* ("I like the way you used red in your painting of your dog"), productivity does not necessarily increase, but their interest does not falter. This means that they will go on working on the tasks on their own initiative, and the disposition to go on working and learning will be strengthened.

The Development of Interest

One of the important dispositions teachers want to cultivate in young children is the development of *interest*. Interest is the capacity to lose oneself in an activity or concern outside of oneself. It also refers to the capacity to become deeply enough absorbed in something to pursue it over time and with sufficient commitment to accept the routine aspects involved in carrying out the task. This disposition appears to be present at birth in the form of the orienting response and is affected by a variety of social-psychological processes throughout childhood. But there are many obstacles to maintaining and strengthening the interest disposition in our television age where things occur in short bursts of time.

Effects of Rewards and Feedback on Interest

Recent research has illuminated the effects of rewards on children's interest disposition toward given activities. The pleasure or satisfaction derived from an activity that a child undertakes voluntarily is thought to be its own justification. Research on the so-called *over-justification effect* suggests that when children are rewarded for activities they initially showed spontaneous interest in, their interest in those activities is reduced (Deci and Ryan 1985). Thus when a reward is offered, the activity is said to be "over" justified. This research suggests that a principle of practice is for teachers to exercise care not to offer re-

children in such programs could best be described as "time on deadly task." After a year or two of such schooling, the cumulative effect on the disposition to learn is likely to be stultifying!

Learned Stupidity

Another risk of introducing young children to academic work prematurely is that those children who cannot relate to the content or tasks required are likely to feel incompetent. When the content of a lecture for college students is difficult to grasp, students are very likely to fault the instructor — as many of us well know! However, with young children the cumulative effect of repeated failure in doing assigned tasks is likely to be the self-message, "I am stupid." This self-attribution of stupidity is "learned stupidity." Such children are then likely to behave in a manner consistent with this self-attribution, even on occasions when they might have been able to succeed in the task.

Informal Learning Environment

Another principle of practice in designing curricula for young children is that the younger the children are, the more informal the learning environment should be, with the larger portion of their time allocated to informal activities. There are two kinds of informality. One is spontaneous play, in which materials, props, and equipment are available for children to play with spontaneously. These might include the dress-up corner, block building, painting, sand and water play, and so on. The other kind of informality is when children are interacting as they work together to make things, pursue a topic, or do a project.

used should optimize the acquisition of knowledge, skills, *and* desirable dispositions and feelings. All four categories of learning should be adopted as mutually inclusive goals, with each category having equal weight. It is clearly not very useful to have skills if, in the process of acquiring them, the disposition to use them is lost. On the other hand, having a disposition without the requisite skills also is not a desirable educational outcome.

Teachers of young children do not have an either/or choice: either to teach academic skills *or* to cultivate desirable dispositions. The challenge for educators − at every level − is to help the learner with *both* acquisition of skills and strengthening the dispositions that will give rise to their use. Curriculum planning must take into account the development of knowledge, skills, dispositions, and appropriate feelings as mutually inclusive goals.

Variety of Teaching Methods

Another risk for preschool programs that emphasize academic or basic skills is that they tend to use a single teaching approach. Academically focused curricula typically adopt a single pedagogical method dominated by basal reader teacher's manuals, workbooks, drill, and practice. When a single teaching method is used with children who are diverse in background, development, and experiences, it is likely that a significant proportion of them will fail. A principle of practice is that the younger the children, the greater the variety of teaching methods that should be employed. The younger the group, the less likely they are to have been socialized into a standard way of responding to instruction; their readiness to learn is unique and idiosyncratic rather than common and shared.

For reasons of practicality, there are, of course, limits as to how varied teaching methods can be. Methods that are dominated by workbooks, worksheets, and drill, which claim to individualize instruction, typically individualize only the day on which a given child completes a set task, not the task itself! Too often "time on task" for

Risks of Academic Pressures on Young Children

Observation of young children in many preschool settings indicates that they can learn by rote some aspects of phonics, counting, and other academic tasks. But as pointed out earlier, the fact that children *can* do something is not sufficient justification for requiring it of them. While there is no compelling evidence to suggest that early introduction to academic work guarantees success in school in the long term, there is ample evidence to show that it could be counterproductive.

Certainly, young children can be successfully instructed in beginning reading skills; however, the risk is that, given the amount of drill and practice required to succeed in these skills at an early age, children's dispositions to be readers may be jeopardized. Of course, there are some young children who spontaneously express a real desire to learn to read. They should be supported in their efforts to do so in a matter-of-fact way, not in a way that leads them to think they are superior to classmates less ready to read.

Direct instruction of young children to perform academic tasks (practice in phonics, workbook exercises) may appear harmless, or even beneficial, in the short term (Katz and Chard, forthcoming). But educators are obliged to take into account the potential long-term consequences of pressuring young children to perform academic tasks, no matter how benign they appear to be at the time. Results from longitudinal studies suggest that the curriculum and teaching methods

able say to themselves something like, "Am I going to show again that I don't have much ability?" or "How can I avoid being judged by others as not having sufficient ability?" They tend to become anxious, and their anxiety often contributes to deterioration of their performance.

When teachers set tasks that emphasize learning rather than performance goals, they might say to children something like: "Today I want to see how much you can find out about X," or "Your assignment is to learn as much as you can about Y." With the stress on learning, children tend to see opportunities to achieve something, whatever their ability. They tend to ask of themselves, "What do I have to do?" or "What do I need in order to find out about X?" rather than "Do I have enough ability?" The research indicates that when performance goals are imposed, children tend to become ego-oriented and worry about how they will be judged. With learning goals, they tend to become task-oriented; and the disposition to make an effort is strengthened. Furthermore, children with a strong orientation to performance goals come to believe that real effort reflects low ability, while little effort indicates high ability (Dweck 1986). High ability is reflected in the expression, "no sweat!"

Children cannot all be equal in ability. Some children are more mathematically able than others; some are more musical, more verbal, or more athletic than others. These differences maximize what children can do together. Therefore, in setting tasks for children we ought to say much more often than we do, "See how much you and Mary can find out about X," rather than, "How many can you get right?"

There are many dispositions that we want children to acquire and strengthen: to be curious, creative, cooperative, friendly, helpful, hard working, and resourceful, to name a few. The disposition to be inquisitive cannot be strengthened by instruction, order, command, or hearing lectures about it. Dispositions are probably learned primarily from being around people who have them and who exhibit them. Unfortunately, too few adults exhibit a disposition like curiosity in front of children. How often do we hear an adult or even a teacher say, "I've been wondering if this is the best way to do such and such," or "I must find out how X really works"?

Another means of strengthening desired dispositions is to acknowledge and express appreciation of them when they are exhibited. For example, if in the course of listening to a story, a child expresses curiosity about a particular topic in the story, the teacher might return the next day with some pertinent information, books, or pictures on the topic. In doing this, the teacher acknowledges the child's interest by following up on it the next day. Acknowledgment of and appreciative responses to desirable dispositions are not the same as extrinsic rewards or even praise. The latter distract children from the disposition-related behavior; acknowledgment and appreciation reinforce the behavior and encourage the child to continue to manifest the disposition and to pursue the activity in which it is expressed.

Recent research on children's motivation suggests another consideration in strengthening children's intellectual dispositions. It concerns the way teachers set tasks for their students. For instance, if a teacher says to the class, "Today, I want to see how good you are at X," or "I want to see how many you can get Y right," the teacher is setting performance goals. The research indicates that children typically respond to such performance goal tasks with concern about whether they have the ability to perform successfully (Dweck and Leggett 1988). Under performance goal conditions, highly able children tend to say to themselves, "Good, I can show how smart I am again today." On the other hand, children who do not see themselves as highly

to want to know more, to be inquisitive or "nosey." Friendliness and unfriendliness are dispositions. Creativity is probably a set of dispositions. Bossiness is a disposition. Not all dispositions are desirable, by any means.

The distinction between skills and dispositions becomes clearer when we think about the difference between having reading skills and having the disposition to be a reader, or having writing skills and having the disposition to be a writer. Possessing a particular skill does not automatically guarantee that the owner has the disposition to employ it.

Feelings. The fourth category of learning is feelings. Feelings are subjective emotional states. Most are probably innate; the rudimentary capacities to feel fear, anger, affection, love, contentment, and other basic emotional responses are most likely present at birth. But feelings associated with particular events and phenomena are learned from experience and from interacting with significant others. There are many feelings that concern us as educators: feelings of confidence, competence, and security, to name a few. Children's feelings of belonging, acceptance, or rejection are important to parents as well as to educators.

Fostering the Four Categories of Learning

Knowledge is acquired primarily through interaction with knowledgeable others (Bruner and Haste 1987). It is acquired when others share what they know, when they explain or tell something, and when they alert children to significant events around them. Only a relatively small proportion of children's knowledge is acquired through trial-and-error and discovery processes. Knowledge is strengthened by study and repetition.

Skills can be learned through observation, by instruction, or by trial and error. Appropriate directions and coaching also can help with skill acquisition. Skills can be strengthened with the right amount and the right kind of drill and practice.

Dispositions are not learned the same way as knowledge and skills. They are not learned through instruction, drill, lectures, or workbooks.

Four Categories of Learning

While there are many kinds of learning of interest to educators, I find it helpful when dealing with young children to focus on four broad categories of learning: knowledge, skills, dispositions, and feelings. Each category is defined briefly below followed by a discussion of how the learning in each category can be fostered.

Knowledge. This category of learning is of concern to educators at every level. The nature of knowledge varies with the age, experience, and expertise of the individual. For young children, knowledge includes such elements as simple facts, concepts, names of things in the environment, stories, myths, songs, and many other items of culturally shared information.

Skills. Skills are small units of action; they can be easily observed and are executed in a relatively short period of time. It would take many pages to list all the skills to be learned in early childhood. The more specific we are in describing the skills, the longer the list would become. They include physical, perceptual, and social skills; verbal and conversational skills; handwriting skills; counting skills; and many more.

Dispositions. Dispositions are a very different category of learning from knowledge and skills. A disposition can be thought of as a habit of mind or a tendency to respond to classes of situations in a certain way. For example, curiosity is a disposition. It is neither a skill nor an item of knowledge. It refers to an habitual tendency

they have observed through talk and pictures. In doing these things, they can apply whatever skills they already have, use emerging skills, and acquire new ones. Young children should be interacting with adults and with each other, with materials, and with their environment in ways that help them to make sense of their own experience. The relevant principle of practice here is that with increasing age and experience, children can be asked to make sense of other people's environments and experiences — those far away in place and time.

In addition to learning through trial and error and by observation, young children gain a great deal, cognitively as well as socially, in the course of interacting with each other, with adults, and with aspects of their environment. One of the risks of having the conventional academic tasks pushed down from the primary grades is that it reduces the opportunities for young children to engage in the kinds of active and interactive intellectual and social processes through which so much can be learned.

Furthermore, even though young children initially are eager to participate in frivolous and meaningless tasks at the beginning of their school careers, their novelty soon wears off. Some children stay with them longer than others; but the cumulative effect of repeated exposure to such tasks may be boredom, disillusionment, and disappointment with school and learning. It should not be surprising, then, that a few children will attempt to enliven the school setting in ways that are beneficial neither to them nor to their classmates.

The developmental principle at issue is not simply when or how children learn: children will always learn. They learn to lie, to steal, to like or dislike school, to compete or cooperate, to trust or to mistrust — depending on their experiences and the cumulative effects they produce. Humans are not born liking or disliking school or mathematics. While it is not necessary for children to love these things, it is imperative that they find them *interesting* and *mind-engaging*. The developmental question, then, is not what young children can do but what should young children do that best serves their development in the long term.

The Role of Interactive Learning

Over and over again, contemporary research tells us that learning for young children is maximized when they are engaged in interaction. Recent interest and research in the seminal ideas of Vygotsky (Wertsch 1985) confirm the view that young children learn best by direct and firsthand interaction with people and objects in their environment, and that they should be engaged in active rather than passive activities (See Katz and Chard, forthcoming). This is why it is better to start young children with writing before introducing them to reading. Writing is an expressive and active activity, while reading is a receptive and passive one. It is not necessary that we be able to read their writing (Wells 1988); they will interpret or translate for you.

Young children should be making and building things, observing worthwhile events and phenomena around them, and recording what

example, exposure to violence in films and television might be harmless if it occurs rarely; but the cumulative effects of frequent exposure appear to be an indifference to violence and the suffering it causes (Tuchscherer 1988).

While the normative dimension tells us what most children can and cannot do at a given age, the dynamic dimension tells us what young children should do in light of the dynamic long-term effects of early experience on later functioning. Taken together, these two major dimensions of development suggest that just because young children can do something does not mean they should do it. It is well established within cultures and across cultures that young children can engage in a very wide variety of behavior. For example, in developing countries it is common to see children at the age of six and seven engaged in child rearing, raising their siblings who are two and three, sometimes even younger. The fact that it can be done does not mean that it should be done − or that it should not be done. Much depends on how a community defines its behavorial norms and ultimate goals.

In many day-care centers and kindergartens, young children can be seen filling out worksheets or "reading" from flash cards. Certainly young children can be coerced into rote counting of numbers and participating in daily reading drills long before they really comprehend what they mean. Young children can easily be coaxed into working for gold stars, stickers, tokens, and all sorts of extrinsic rewards. But just because they can do so, does not mean they should.

Because young children are so trusting and eager to please their teachers, they willingly do almost any task assigned to them. They rarely appear to be suffering from the frequently meaningless activities provided in many of our preschools and kindergartens; some even appear to enjoy them. However, children's enjoyment of an activity is never a sufficient criterion for its inclusion. Young children enjoy junk food, television shows of doubtful value, and war toys. That does not qualify these items as developmentally appropriate for or potentially beneficial to them.

children. Let us begin with a discussion of the concept of development and categories of learning. This will be followed by some principles of practice that take account of recent knowledge about children's development and learning.

The Concept of Development

The concept of development has two major dimensions. The first is the *normative* dimension, which tells us something about what children can do at a given age or stage, that which is typical or commonly observed in children at two, three, five, or seven. At what age can they be expected to take their first step? How many words might they know at various ages? When people say something is developmentally appropriate, they are usually referring to this normative dimension of development, that is, the typical patterns and norms of developmental progress from birth to maturity.

The second is the *dynamic* dimension. It has three aspects that contribute to our understanding and knowledge of growth. The first has to do with the sequences of learning, the changes and transformations that occur in capabilities from one stage to the next.

The second aspect concerns the delayed impact that early experiences can have on later functioning. Sometimes this is referred to as a "sleeper effect," since it appears to be an early experience that lies dormant for a long period during growth. One example is the common experience many parents have of being surprised, when speaking to their children, at how very much they sound like their own parents — often saying the very things, the very same way that they swore they would never say when they became parents! In this way our early experience as children has a delayed and usually unconscious effect on our mature behavior.

The third aspect of the dynamic dimension concerns the possible cumulative effects of childhood experiences. Many experiences of childhood might be quite harmless if they are occasional or infrequent, but could be damaging if they occur frequently over a long time. For

Implications of Recent Research for the Early Childhood Curriculum

Planning a curriculum for young children involves answering three basic questions. First, *what* kinds of development and learning do we wish to foster? Second, *when* should these learnings be expected and introduced? And third, *how* can they best be accomplished?

The *what* question helps explicate and define the goals of the program. Goals are relatively easy to agree on. There is general consensus in most communities that all children should achieve basic literacy and numeracy, acquire problem-solving skills, develop the capacity to persist in worthwhile tasks, and acquire a taste for learning. It is also generally agreed that the groundwork should be laid for the development of the basic values and competencies associated with responsible citizenship.

The goals of an educational program are set primarily by the clients to be served: the parents and society at large who, in turn, charge educators with the responsibility of achieving the goals as fully as possible. Educators then use their knowledge and understanding of child development to answer the *when* questions about curriculum design. And with their knowledge and understanding of the nature of learning and the principles of pedagogy, they answer the questions about *how* the goals of an educational program can best be achieved.

Fortunately, there is now an abundance of recent research on children's development and learning, which is rich with implications for answering the *when* and *how* questions of program planning for young

tion of State Boards of Education, the National Governors' Association, and the Carnegie Foundation for the Advancement of Teaching have recently identified planning for the needs of young children as a national priority.

Curriculum Trends

Unfortunately, practices in early childhood programs are frequently inconsistent with what we know about children's development. Discrepancies between what we know and what we do show up in several trends that warrant concern. One is the "hot-housing" or "push down" phenomenon in which the academic expectations and curriculum content and methods traditionally used in the first grade are pushed down into the kindergarten and preschool (Gallagher and Coche 1987; Hitz and Wright 1988) It seems to be a matter of doing to children earlier and earlier what probably should not even be done to them later!

Another trend is the establishment of alternative or "transitional" classes for entering or exiting kindergarten children who fall below arbitrary standards on tests of dubious validity (NAEYC 1988). The provision of such special classes reflects the view that the children should "fit" the curriculum; yet current research on children's learning and development suggests that the order should be reversed: the curriculum should be adapted to the characteristics of the children (Katz, Raths, and Torres 1986).

Both of these trends reflect distorted notions of what is appropriate education for young children. Because such practices have become so widespread, the National Association for the Education of Young Children (NAEYC) has felt it necessary to address them by issuing official position statements on both developmentally appropriate practices for young children (Bredekamp 1987) and on standardized testing for young children (NAEYC 1988).

In this fastback, I shall review recent research on young children's learning and discuss the implications of that research for developmentally appropriate early childhood education.

Trends in Early Childhood Education

If current trends in child care and early education continue, most children will spend major portions of their early lives in settings outside of their homes in the next century. The steady increase during the last 20 years in the employment of mothers of young children, and the deepening conviction that appropriate early educational experiences improve children's responsiveness to subsequent schooling are two of the factors underlying these trends.

Kagan (1987) points out that while only 11% of three- and four-year-olds were enrolled in preschools in 1965, the percentage more than tripled to 39% by 1985; and the trend is expected to increase dramatically during this century's last decade. The Center for Education Statistics (1985) estimates that by 1993 about seven million children will be enrolled in some type of preprimary program, and about half of them will be based in public school settings. Day (1988) reports that the percentage of five-year-olds enrolled in kindergarten has increased from 70% in 1970 to about 95% in 1985; and that while most kindergarten children currently are enrolled in half-day programs, the adoption of a longer or full-day kindergarten program is gradually spreading.

Today, the provision of good quality care and education of the nation's young children is a concern not only to parents and educators; it is now among the most urgent topics on the agendas of local, state, and national politicians. Such organizations as the National Associa-